A Calendar of Sonnets

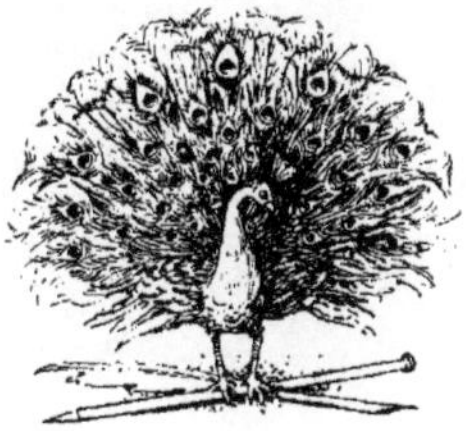

ILLUSTRATIONS.

ne full-page Designs . . . . By EMILÉ BAYARD.

ne Vignettes to the Text . . . . . . By E. H. GARRETT.

Engraving by JOHN ANDREW & SON CO.

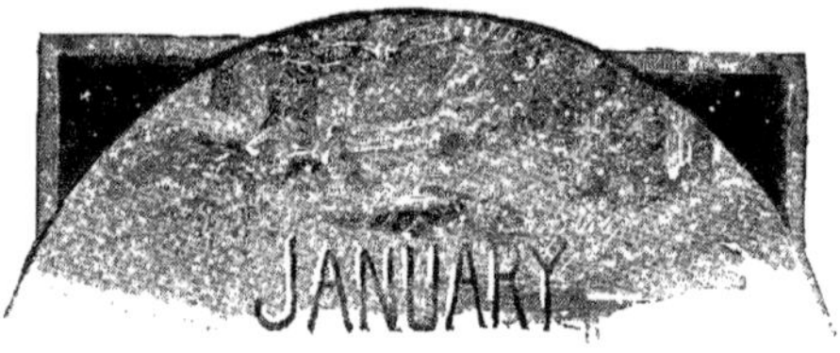
JANUARY

O WINTER! frozen pulse and heart of fire,
What loss is theirs who from thy kingdom turn
Dismayed, and think thy snow a sculptured urn
Of death! Far sooner in midsummer tire
The streams than under ice. June could not hire
Her roses to forego the strength they learn
In sleeping on thy breast. No fires can burn
The bridges thou dost lay where men desire
In vain to build.
O Heart, when Love's sun goes
To northward, and the sounds of singing cease,
Keep warm by inner fires, and rest in peace.
Sleep on content, as sleeps the patient rose.
Walk boldly on the white untrodden snows,
The winter is the winter's own release.

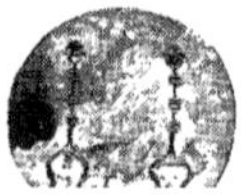

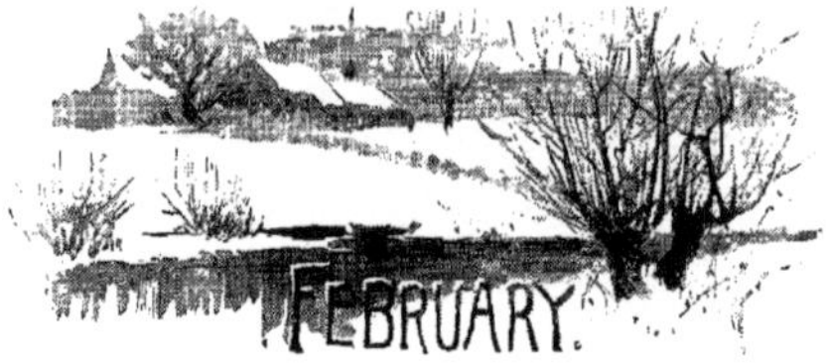
FEBRUARY.

STILL lie the sheltering snows, undimmed and white;
And reigns the winter's pregnant silence still;
No sign of spring, save that the catkins fill,
And willow stems grow daily red and bright.
These are the days when ancients held a rite
Of expiation for the old year's ill,
And prayer to purify the new year's will:
Fit days, ere yet the spring rains blur the sight,
Ere yet the bounding blood grows hot with haste,
And dreaming thoughts grow heavy with a greed
The ardent summer's joy to have and taste;
Fit days, to give to last year's losses heed,
To reckon clear the new life's sterner need;
Fit days, for Feast of Expiation placed!

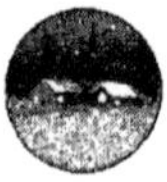

MARCH.

MONTH which the warring ancients strangely styled
　　The month of war,—as if in their fierce ways
Were any month of peace!—in thy rough days
I find no war in Nature, though the wild
Winds clash and clang, and broken boughs are piled
At feet of writhing trees. The violets raise
Their heads without affright, without amaze,
And sleep through all the din, as sleeps a child.
And he who watches well may well discern
Sweet expectation in each living thing.
Like pregnant mother the sweet earth doth yearn;
In secret joy makes ready for the spring;
And hidden, sacred, in her breast doth bear
Annunciation lilies for the year.

APRIL.

: :

APRIL.

NO days such honored days as these! When yet
Fair Aphrodite reigned, men seeking wide
For some fair thing which should forever bide
On earth, her beauteous memory to set
In fitting frame that no age could forget,
Her name in lovely April's name did hide,
And leave it there, eternally allied
To all the fairest flowers Spring did beget.
And when fair Aphrodite passed from earth,
Her shrines forgotten and her feasts of mirth,
A holier symbol still in seal and sign,
Sweet April took, of kingdom most divine,
When Christ ascended, in the time of birth
Of spring anemones, in Palestine.

MAY

O MONTH when they who love must love and wed!
    Were one to go to worlds where May is naught,
And seek to tell the memories he had brought
From earth of thee, what were most fitly said?
I know not if the rosy showers shed
From apple-boughs, or if the soft green wrought
In fields, or if the robin's call be fraught
The most with thy delight. Perhaps they read
Thee best who in the ancient time did say
Thou wert the sacred month unto the old:
No blossom blooms upon thy brightest day
So subtly sweet as memories which unfold
In aged hearts which in thy sunshine lie,
To sun themselves once more before they die.

O MONTH whose promise and fulfilment blend,
    And burst in one! it seems the earth can store
In all her roomy house no treasure more;
Of all her wealth no farthing have to spend
On fruit, when once this stintless flowering end.
And yet no tiniest flower shall fall before
It hath made ready at its hidden core
Its tithe of seed, which we may count and tend
Till harvest. Joy of blossomed love, for thee
Seems it no fairer thing can yet have birth?
No room is left for deeper ecstasy?
Watch well if seeds grow strong, to scatter free
Germs for thy future summers on the earth.
A joy which is but joy soon comes to dearth.

JULY.

SOME flowers are withered and some joys have died;
   The garden reeks with an East Indian scent
From beds where gillyflowers stand weak and spent;
The white heat pales the skies from side to side;
But in still lakes and rivers, cool, content,
Like starry blooms on a new firmament,
White lilies float and regally abide.
In vain the cruel skies their hot rays shed;
The lily does not feel their brazen glare.
In vain the pallid clouds refuse to share
Their dews; the lily feels no thirst, no dread.
Unharmed she lifts her queenly face and head;
She drinks of living waters and keeps fair.

AUGUST

SILENCE again. The glorious symphony
    Hath need of pause and interval of peace.
Some subtle signal bids all sweet sounds cease,
Save hum of insects' aimless industry.
Pathetic summer seeks by blazonry
Of color to conceal her swift decrease.
Weak subterfuge! Each mocking day doth fleece
A blossom, and lay bare her poverty.
Poor middle-agèd summer! Vain this show!
Whole fields of golden-rod cannot offset
One meadow with a single violet :
And well the singing thrush and lily know,
Spite of all artifice which her regret
Can deck in splendid guise, their time to go!

September

O GOLDEN month! How high thy gold is heaped!
The yellow birch-leaves shine like bright coins strung
On wands; the chestnut's yellow pennons tongue
To every wind its harvest challenge. Steeped
In yellow, still lie fields where wheat was reaped;
And yellow still the corn sheaves, stacked among
The yellow gourds, which from the earth have wrung
Her utmost gold. To highest boughs have leaped
The purple grape, — last thing to ripen, late
By very reason of its precious cost.
O Heart, remember, vintages are lost
If grapes do not for freezing night-dews wait.
Think, while thou sunnest thyself in Joy's estate,
Mayhap thou canst not ripen without frost!

OCTOBER

THE month of carnival of all the year,
  When Nature lets the wild earth go its way
And spend whole seasons on a single day.
The spring-time holds her white and purple dear;
October, lavish, flaunts them far and near;
The summer charily her reds doth lay
Like jewels on her costliest array;
October, scornful, burns them on a bier.
The winter hoards his pearls of frost in sign
Of kingdom: whiter pearls than winter knew,
Or Empress wore, in Egypt's ancient line,
October, feasting 'neath her dome of blue,
Drinks at a single draught, slow filtered through
Sunshiny air, as in a tingling wine!

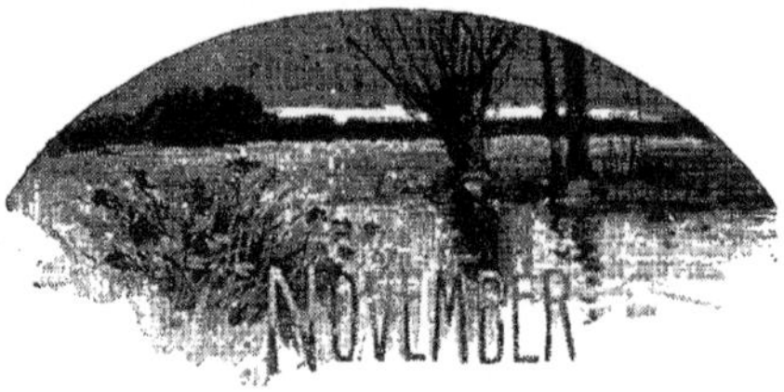
NOVEMBER

THIS is the treacherous month when autumn days
With summer's voice come bearing summer's gifts.
Beguiled, the pale down-trodden aster lifts
Her head and blooms again. The soft, warm haze
Makes moist once more the sere and dusty ways,
And, creeping through where dead leaves lie in drifts,
The violet returns. Snow noiseless sifts
Ere night, an icy shroud, which morning's rays
Will idly shine upon and slowly melt,
Too late to bid the violet live again.
The treachery, at last, too late, is plain;
Bare are the places where the sweet flowers dwelt.
What joy sufficient hath November felt?
What profit from the violet's day of pain?

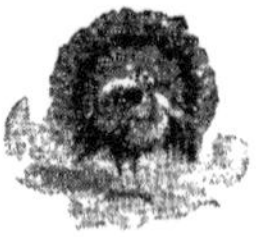

Lightning Source UK Ltd.
Milton Keynes UK
UKHW022248011122
411473UK00003B/276